OR SO

She thought

OR SO

She thought

A story of resilience

SOPHIA WELLS

PALMETTO
P U B L I S H I N G
Charleston, SC
www.PalmettoPublishing.com

Paperback ISBN: 979-8-8229-4725-2

❖

To my husband, whose unwavering love and support sustained me through the darkest days. You are my rock, and I am forever grateful for your presence in my life.

To my therapist, who believed in me when I couldn't believe in myself and guided me toward healing. Your patience, compassion, and encouragement empowered me to reclaim my strength and rewrite my story.

To my family, for their endless love, understanding, and patience as I embarked on this journey of self discovery and healing. Your unwavering support gave me courage to face my demons and embrace my truth.

This book is a testament to the love and resilience of my husband, my therapist, and my family. Thank you all for hopping on the trauma train.

Based on a true story.

In quiet the corridors of her past, amidst the echoes of pain and the whispers of resilience, meet Belle. As she navigates the shadows of multiple traumas, join her on a journey where the strength within her flickers like a beacon, guiding her from the darkest nights to the dawn of triumph. This is her story a testament to the indescribable spirit that emerges when one faces life's stories with courage, determination, and unwavering will to rewrite the narrative of her own existence.

Content Warning:
This story contains themes of assault, trauma,
suicidal ideation, and addiction.

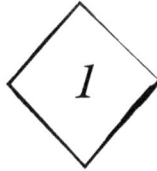

1

Belle

In the intricate railroads of her existence, Belle steered through life's tracks. Encountering adversities like relentless oncoming trains, she found peace and wisdom in the embrace of her grandparents. Their stories became the backdrop of her upbringing, shaping her identity with every tale they shared. Little did she know that beneath the familiar warmth of their love lay a revelation that would redefine her understanding of family.

Her story unfolds like a train's journey, with stops at stations of sorrow and trauma where she faces winds that could have derailed a weaker spirit. As her journey was just starting, a knock at her front door would reveal her first loss. Belle lost her lifelong best friend in a horrific car accident. She was only eight years old. Continuing on through her young years, a startling truth emerged her father, Dale, the figure she had long regarded as her bloodline, was not her biological father. This revelation sent derailments though the tracks of her existence. Struggling with the balance of familial bonds, her identity and belonging, the strength of her grandparents' love became the engine, offering her stability.

❖

Belle lived a typical teenage life. Nothing out of the ordinary. She had two homes. One nested in a City by the Lake and one with True Grit and Amazing Grace.

The City by the Lake, as the locals call it, was an up-and-coming town full of typical small-town politics. Though not always pristine, this home was a sanctuary of love and acceptance, for the most part. The home included well-worn furniture and a lingering smell of cigarettes. True Grit and Amazing Grace was also a small town, but Belle didn't have to compete for friendships here. The home was a bastion of discipline and aspirations. Both suburbs outside of Nashville, Tennessee. Two homes, disparate yet equally significant, each shaping a young girl's understanding of love, responsibility, and the diverse textures of family life.

Belle played a variety of sports. From soccer and softball to basketball. Weeknights filled her schedule with practices and late dinners. Weekends were filled with tournaments and deciding which home she would pick to lay her head. Usually, her decision was based on what was for dinner that evening.

In her teenage years, Belle spent most of her nights out with friends from both towns. As she and her friends prepared for a night out, you could hear boy bands playing from her CD player. As she sat on the floor to apply her makeup and straighten her perfect blond hair, the girls would determine if they were either gathering in the Food Lion parking lot; or watching the boys play volleyball at the courts. The smell of Love Spell and hairspray filled the room as they completed the final step.

She graduated with honors a few months after her grandmother's death. At the young age of eighteen, Belle had already lost two important people in her life. She was ready to be on her own. Belle enrolled at the local community college.

In the crisp embrace of a fall day in 2006, as an eighteen year-old girl navigating the halls of a community college, the campus was filled with laughter and hues of red and black. The trees were still green with jealousy, as fall in middle Tennessee isn't really fall. It was a crisp ninety degrees as Belle made her way to class.

The air was infused with humidity, and the ground was crunchy from the lack of rain in the area. Around the courtyard, fellow students gathered together in denim skirts, layered tank tops, and flair-legged pants. The click-clack of flip phones and iPods, complete with chunky headphones, provided the soundtrack to the scene.

Between classes, the students were lounging at community tables in the courtyards or waiting in line at the McDonald's across the street. Friendships were built of shared dreams and the challenges of early adulthood. Belle gave it her best. Even though her thoughts were filled with déjà vu. She had been the first one in her family to go to college, but this was like an overpriced high school.

A semester later, Belle decided to drop out. She told her mom and grandpa that it was just for a semester, but; she knew this wasn't the path for her. As Belle started to go her own way, she was given a promotion to manger at the local tanning salon.

The scent of tanning lotions, infused with tropical and coconut fragrance, lingered in the air; soft music and the hum of tanning beds created a soothing ambiance. Belle was independently making a life for herself.

Belle's journey into medical school was a testament to her determination and growth as a young adult. Taking a few years to explore life and develop a deeper understanding of herself allowed her to enter medical school with a sense of purpose and maturity.

It was during her time in medical school that Belle's path crossed with Adam's. As a family friend, she had always known Adam to be a significant presence in her life, but she never anticipated the pivotal role he would come to play.

The reunion in the parking lot of a local mall sparked a connection that transcended their previous acquaintance. As she embarked on her respective journey toward becoming a healthcare professional, their bond deepened, and Belle found herself drawn to Adam in ways she hadn't expected.

Despite the uncertainties of life and the twists and turns it might bring, Belle couldn't shake the feeling that Adam was meant to be a part of her future. Little did she know that their friendship would evolve into something much more profound, leading them down a path toward marriage and a lifetime of shared dreams.

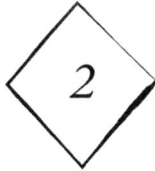

2

Adam

Adam had known Belle for years, watching her grow into a determined young woman. As a family friend, he had always admired her from afar, but it wasn't until they crossed paths in the local mall parking lot that he truly saw her in a new light.

Observing Belle navigate the challenges of medical school with grace and determination, Adam could not help but be captivated by her intellect and dedication to her studies.

He carried the weight of unseen scars, a silent testament to the battles he'd faced. The lines on his face told stories of both joy and struggle, yet his loyalty to Belle's family remained unwavering. Also hurt by life's twists, he didn't let his pain tarnish his relationships.

Having been raised by his grandparents, like Belle, he understood what it is to be a southern gentleman. He embodied a blend of manners, charm, and hospitality that reflected his traditions. His speech was marked by politeness and genuine warmth.

Adam privately struggled with addiction. The pain inflicted by loved ones in his past was too much to bear at times. Taking a pill to silence the pain, he sought refuge in the numbness it promised. In the quiet solitude that followed, the act dulled, but the echoes of a traumatic childhood still remained. The pills offered a temporary high, a delicate balance between relief and the awareness that the true source of healing lay beyond the grasp of a pill.

Adam was taken away by the beauty of Belle. He saw something in her. Something that needed saving. He wouldn't know until many years later that they would be saving each other.

Still being a loyal friend, Adam wanted to ask permission to take Belle out for dinner. He nervously adjusted his tie as he stood outside the door to Dale's office, rehearsing his words for what felt like the hundredth time. Today, he was determined to ask Belle's father permission to take her out on a date. Taking a deep breath, Adam approached the door and knocked gently. The door swung open, revealing Belle's father, Dale, a stern yet kind-hearted man.

"Adam, what brings you here?" Dale greeted him with a curious expression. They were close friends; why was he suddenly knocking?

"Good Morning, Dale," Adam began, his voice wavering slightly. "I hope you are doing well today. I've come here to ask for your permission to take Belle on a date."

Dale's eyebrows raised in surprise, but he maintained his composed demeanor. "A date, huh? Well, I appreciate your honesty; come on in."

Adam followed Dale into his office, where Dale called Kathy.

"Adam has something he'd like to discuss with us," Dale announced, gesturing for Adam to take a seat.

With a nervous gulp, Adam explained his intentions to them, emphasizing his respect for Belle and his desire to treat her with the utmost care and consideration.

As he spoke, Adam couldn't help but steal glances at Dale, searching for any sign of approval or disapproval. To his relief, Dale listened intently, nodding occasionally as Adam spoke. Once Adam had finished, there was a brief silence as Dale and Kathy communicated silently.

"Well, Adam," Dale finally spoke, his voice calm yet firm. "It's clear that you care deeply for Belle, and we appreciate your honesty. We trust that you will treat her with the respect that she deserves."

Adam's heart soared with relief as Dale gave him his blessing. He couldn't wait to share the news with Belle to begin planning their special evening together. Leaving work that evening, Adam felt a newfound sense of confidence and excitement. With Dale's permission secured, he was ready to take Belle on a date she wouldn't soon forget.

Later that night, Adam looked up Belle on Facebook. He sent her a simple DM.

Adam: "Hey."

Belle: "Hey you."

Adam: "I know we have known each other for several years but I wanted to know if you wanted to grab a bite to eat this weekend?"

Belle: "Absolutely, let me ask my parents."

Adam: "They know, I already asked their permission."

❖

Adam's experience with drug addiction sheds a light on the harsh reality of a crisis that emerged in recent years. In the past, medical professionals often prescribed narcotics with little caution, inadvertently contributing to the widespread addiction that ensued.

Adam's story is a poignant example of how easily one can fall into the trap of dependency. His multiple knee surgeries, stemming from a childhood condition, exposed him to potent painkillers that provided temporary relief but ultimately because a crutch for deeper emotional struggles he had yet to confront.

As the opioids offered relief from physical pain, they also provided a numbing effect on Adam's unresolved mental health issues. However, what was a means of coping soon spiraled into a full-blown addiction, trapping him in a cycle of dependence and despair. You will see that Adam's mourning serves as a stark reminder of the complexities surrounding addiction and the need for a more holistic approach to healthcare. It underscores the importance of not only addressing the physical ailments but providing support for mental well-being to prevent individuals like Adam from slipping through the cracks of a broken system.

3

The First Date

Adam's tires went over the small curb to pull into the driveway. Belle was already on the porch, waiting with excitement. The anticipation of being alone with Belle, coupled with the desire to make a good impression, created a flood of emotions. Is *she* the one? Is *he* the one?

Belle suggested that they go for a drive. Driving down a backroad in the summer feels like an escape. The warm breeze blows your hair as the vibrant greenery on either side of the road dances in the moonlight. The open windows invite the scent of blooming flowers and the fresh air, creating a sensory symphony. As the road stretched ahead, inviting them on an adventure, they started to learn slowly about one another.

"Favorite color?" Adam asked.

"Pink. You?"

"I am color blind, but Blue."

"Really?!" Belle was surprised, because Adam was always so well dressed. How does he know what color shirt matches? Does he see me like I see me?

Their date continued in a parking lot with an intimate and cozy feeling. The soft glow of the dashboard lights created a warm ambiance as they embarked on this date together. Conversation continued to flow easily, punctuated by shared laughter and stolen glances. The car became a private haven, creating a sense of closeness that they both desired. An unfolding connection between the two of them began.

As Belle and Adam continued to date, their bond grew stronger with each passing day. What started as timid conversations and nervous glances soon blossomed into deep conversations filled with laughter and shared dreams. Their dates became more adventurous as they explored new places together, from cozy cafes to scenic drives in the country. With each experience they discovered more about each other, uncovering shared interests and hidden quirks that made them fall even deeper in love.

Belle marveled at Adam's kindness and thoughtfulness, while Adam admired Belle's intelligence and unwavering compassion for others. They found comfort in each other's presence, knowing that they could be themselves without fear of judgment.

As they spent more time together, Belle and Adam opened their hearts to one another, sharing their hopes, fears, and aspirations for the future. They supported each other through challenges, offering a shoulder to lean on and a listening ear whenever needed. Before they knew it, Belle and Adam found themselves falling head over heels in love. It was as if they were meant to be together, two puzzle pieces that fit perfectly side by side.

Their love was evident to everyone around them, radiating warmth and joy wherever they went. Friends and family cheered them on as they embarked on this journey of love, knowing that Belle and Adam were destined for happiness together.

As they continued to date, their love only grew stronger, solidifying their bond and reminding them that they were each other's greatest treasure. Belle and Adam had found true love in each other, and their hearts were forever intertwined in a love story that would last a lifetime.

4

First Five Years

July 7, 2009. Their firstborn son, Wyatt, entered the world. The excitement between the three of them was unmatched.

Wyatt was a very intelligent boy. He met each milestone early. Walking at only eleven months old, he was able to almost say "Mama."

Before Wyatt had been born, Adam had accepted a job a few hours away. The three of them had spent every weekend together, learning the roads of Chattanooga, Tennessee.

Belle and Adam agreed that it was time for their family to be together. They rented a townhome in Chattanooga. These first five years of their relationship included a love-filled engagement, a wedding of Belle's dreams, and a honeymoon for the books. Their marriage included a dynamic blend of discovery, growth, and shared experiences. They were excited to build their life together, navigating any challenges and learning each other's quirks. They learned to build a foundation of trust. During this time, Adam hid his addiction well. Belle honestly had no clue. He was the man that she had always dreamed of. The man that took care of all the finances. He was the provider that she needed.

As the morning sun bathes the rolling hills of Tennessee in a golden glow, the city of Chattanooga awakens to the promise of another day filled with adventure and discovery. Nestled in a verdant valley, cradled by the majestic Tennessee River, and embraced by the ancient peaks of Lookout Mountain, Chattanooga beckons travelers with its irresistible blend of natural beauty, rich history, and vibrant culture.

In the heart of downtown, the pulse of the city thrums with energy as bustling streets lined with red-brick buildings hum with activity. Here, the echoes of their city's storied past mingle with the rhythm of modern life, creating a tapestry of sights, sounds, and experiences that captivate the senses.

Venturing beyond the city limits, the landscape unfolds like a living canvas, each stroke greener, and granite a testament to the natural wonders that abound. Lookout Mountain, Adam and Belle's favorite place rises majestically on the horizon, its rugged cliffs and emerald forests beckoning adventures to explore its hidden depths. Here, amidst the caverns of Ruby Falls and the panoramic views of Rock City, they were always transported to a realm of awe and wonder, where nature's beauty knows no bounds.

But to them, Chattanooga was more than just a haven for outdoor activities. It was a magical place, a sanctuary for the soul, where the past met the present and dreams took flight on the wings of imagination. And so, as the stars twinkled overhead and the lights of the city began to dance, one thing became clear: in Chattanooga, the journey was just beginning.

5

Living with an Addict

As the sun rose over the quiet suburban neighborhood; of her home-
town, Belle awakened to the harsh reality of another day clouded
by the shadow of her husband's addiction. The familiar ache in her
chest served as a constant reminder of the pain that had become an
unwelcome companion in their lives. With a heavy heart, she braced
herself for the challenges that lay ahead, knowing that despite her
deepest desires, there was nothing she could do to save the man she
loved from addiction. Adam had promised that he was finished with
the pills. They had discussed trying for another baby, nine years
after having Wyatt. After only a few short months of stopping birth
control, Belle had become pregnant with their second boy, Jackson.

As she prepared breakfast for her children, Belle's thoughts
drifted to the countless nights spent lying awake, consumed by
fear and uncertainty. She recalled the promises made and broken,
the lies whispered in the darkness, and the desperate pleas for him
to seek help echoing in the emptiness of their shared space. With

each passing day the weight of her burden grew heavier, and yet she remained steadfast in her determination to stand by his side, no matter the cost.

Throughout the day, Belle went through the motions of her daily routine, her outward façade betraying the turmoil and rage within. She smiled and nodded, engaged in conversation, and tended to the needs of her family, all the while wrestling with the silent screams of anguish that threatened to consume her from within. Behind closed doors, she wept for the man her husband had once been, mourned the dreams they had once shared, and prayed for a miracle that might never come.

As evening fell and the world outside grew quiet, Belle found herself alone with her thoughts once more. In the silence of their home, she confronted the painful truth that despite her unwavering love and devotion, she could not save her husband from his addiction. The realization weighed heavily over her weary heart.

And yet, as the stars twinkled overhead and the night stretched out before her, Belle found solace in the knowledge that she was not alone. In the embrace of her family and the support of her friends, she found the strength to carry on, to hope for a brighter tomorrow, and to believe that love had the power to conquer even the darkest of nights. For in the depths of her pain, Belle discovered that sometimes, the greatest act of love is simply to hold on and never let go.

Over the years, the silence that Adam was dealing with became quite loud. There were multiple times when Adam said he would stay sober. He didn't. Living with an addict is something that is not discussed in America. Hell, is it discussed anywhere? It is an emotional rollercoaster that never stops. It has moments of hope. It has moments of despair. It has moments of hate and moments of love. But on a cool summer day, Belle and Adam promised to God that they wouldn't give up. Ever.

❖

There are several stories about being an addict, and they all end in one of two ways. Recovery or death. Belle had to live both. The stories of addicts are as diverse as the person. In every story, there are moments of despair, rock bottom, and the climb toward recovery. It takes a village to raise children with a spouse in active recovery.

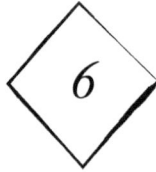

6

2020

It was a normal day for a happy family. Until Wyatt expressed that he was having thoughts of self-harm. They immediately set an appointment for help. This is what Belle thought was the worst day of her life. Or so she thought.

The doctor immediately told them that they were going to Admit him for a seventy-two hour psych-hold. As Belle drove him to the children's hospital, she thought of everything that she had done wrong. What could she have done differently to prevent this?

This is where they learned about the mental health system. At the beginning of 2020, there were only a handful of beds for boys in the state and the same amount for girls. They were all full. His doctors consulted them about sending him to an out-of-state clinic. This is not what they wanted. Their support system was here, in Nashville.

In the sterile hospital room, Belle, a worried mother, felt the chill in the air as she stayed by her eleven-year-old son's side. Adam, at home with Jackson, constantly checked in on his family, as he agreed Wyatt needed his mother. The fluorescent lights cast a clinical glow, reflecting the reality that they faced. Wyatt, struggling with self-harm, engaged in therapeutic games, providing fleeting moments of distraction. The numerous therapy sessions were both a lifeline and a reminder of the struggle they were navigating. Belle found solace in the small moments, trying to bring warmth to the cold hospital room. She did what any mother would, never left his side.

❖

Wyatt's struggle with suicidal thoughts sheds light on the pervasive issue of bullying in today's society. In an age where social media and digital connectivity dominate, bullying can occur at any corner, both in person and online. Boys, in particular, often face challenges with self-esteem, exacerbated by societal expectations and norms.

The constant barrage of social media and the incessant use of cell phones and the internet have created a breeding ground for bullying, making it difficult for individuals like Wyatt to escape its reach.

For Wyatt, the onslaught of bullying and negative-self-perception became overwhelming, driving him to contemplate taking his own life. His experience underscores the urgent need for greater awareness and support systems to address mental health issues in young boys and provide them with the tools to navigate the complexities of modern-day adolescence.

As a society, it is crucial that we recognize the unique challenges boys face in terms of confidence and mental well-being and work toward fostering a culture of acceptance, empathy, and support. By addressing the root causes of bullying and promoting positive self-image and resilience, we can create a safer and more nurturing environment for all young individuals to thrive.

❖

The year 2020 was the year that just kept giving. Just as hundreds of thousands of families were dealing with hardships, so were Belle and Adam.

They purchased their forever home in March of 2020. They spent hours with both kids, remodeling every square inch of the new home. They built memories with their boys. They were happy. Adam was sober and working the program. He had a sponsor. Life was finally getting back on track.

That is until September, when Belle got a call she never thought she would get. She was doing yard work with Adam and Jackson. Adam's mother, Linda, called. She stated that Wyatt had fallen and hit his head. They needed to come to her house immediately. She had been a registered nurse for over twenty years, and something just didn't sit right. Call it mothers's gut. It was a lingering knot in Belle's stomach that she couldn't quite shake. Her instincts were on high alert. Her heart was beating out of her chest.

Belle called Linda for clarification.

"Linda, what has happened with Wyatt?"

"Belle, you need to get here right now. He has fallen down an embankment in the woods and is laying in a creek bed. We have called an ambulance. I–I can't get down there to him."

Belle immediately fell to her knees, screaming in pain. Yep. Today was the worst day of her life. Or so she thought.

A twelve-mile drive took only ten minutes. When they pulled onto Linda's road, there were so many emergency vehicles that they had to park at the end of the street. Belle took off running, screaming, "Where is he???" to all the neighbors standing outside, trying to search for words for what had happened only a short time ago. Belle made it to the embankment; Adam was only a few steps behind her. She was not physically able to get down to her boy. Her firstborn. Adam forces her to sit on the side of the embankment as he headed down with the first responders.

Once he got to Wyatt, he yelled up over one hundred feet from the creek bed.

"Babe, babe, he's okay. He's awake. He's talking."

"Can he move?" Belle called.

"He can feel his hands and toes."

Belle could feel her heart racing. Perched on the edge of the embankment, she viewed the unsettling landscape. The once-welcoming woods now seemed cloaked in shadows, casting an eerie darkness. The rustling leaves echoed with the ominous undertones of first responders. The trees lining the embankment became an entangled maze, heightening the sense of fear and uncertainty. The air felt heavy, carrying an unidentifiable tension that hung over the paths, making each step a cautionary endeavor.

Fighting through tears, she saw Linda on the other side of the embankment. She was standing with one of the neighbors. They were clearly upset. Belle heard leaves crunching and the sound of her mother's voice. It was different this time. Even though it was quivering with tension and distress, Belle felt a small shift of comfort. Kathy sat beside Belle for what felt like days. She helped Belle up onto her feet, and they started to pace. Kathy wanted to get down to Wyatt. Belle told her it wasn't possible. Finally, they could see the tops of helmets carrying what looked like a bright orange sled.

It took first responders over an hour to get Wyatt out of that creek bed. Belle was able to finally lay eyes on her firstborn. He was clearly terrified. He was awake but not moving.

Belle and Adam agreed to leave Jackson with Adam's parents. They were not able to ride in the helicopter. They placed Wyatt in the back of an ambulance. He was Life Flighted right back to where he had been just earlier in the year.

They had to drive him to a field just a few minutes away. Life Flight was waiting for their arrival. They hopped in the car and headed toward the Children's Hospital. The forty-five-minute drive was terrifying. What were they doing with Wyatt? Was he okay? Why were parents not allowed to be with their kids while they were fighting for their lives?

This was the worst day of her life. Or so she thought.

Wyatt, as always, was the star of the show. He had had a traumatic brain injury. One that would follow him. Local news stations reached out for interviews of their family to talk about that awful day. Thank God, he survived.

7

2021

Adam was really struggling. Belle just couldn't see it. She was so focused on the boys that she let small things slip. He would detox himself a handful of times at home. Money would go missing. Household items were being sold. Belle was numb. She did not understand. She made vows to him. Daily, she would reach down and find something inside to keep going.

July 4, 2021. This was the worst day in Belle's life. Her grandpa, her main man, her Northern Star, passed away peacefully in his sleep. She received the call from Kathy, her mother, that he was gone. Just as the fireworks were starting, Belle fell to her knees again, screaming in the front yard of her home. Everyone knew when she said, "He's gone."

Belle and her grandpa Lewis shared a bond that was unlike any other. From the moment Belle was born, Da had been there for her, a constant source of love, guidance, and laughter throughout her life. He was not just her grandpa; he was her best friend, her confidant, and her rock. As Belle grew up, Da was always by her side, cheering her on at school events, telling stories from his own youth, and imparting invaluable wisdom that shaped her into the person that she was becoming. Whether they were throwing a ball in the front yard or working on his next project in the wood workshop, Belle cherished every moment spent with her beloved grandpa.

But as the years passed, Belle began to notice subtle changes in Da. He would forget things more often, struggling to find the right words, and sometimes becoming confused on what day it was. Concerned, Belle and her family took Da to see a doctor, and the diagnosis was devastating: Alzheimer's disease.

Watching her grandpa decline was heartbreaking for Belle. The man who had always been her pillar of strength was now slipping away before her eyes. But Belle was determined to return the love and care that Da had given her throughout her life. With the support of Adam, Kathy, and her husband, Eldrick, Belle dedicated herself to caring for her grandpa in the most loving and compassionate way possible. Together they created a warm and nurturing environment where Da felt safe and loved, even as his memory continued to fade. They surrounded him with familiar photographs, comforting music, and cherished mementos from his past, helping to spark moments of clarity and joy amidst the confusion of Alzheimer's. They took turns reading to him and reminiscing about happy memories from the years gone by. Through it all, Belle never lost sight of the man her grandpa once was, the strong kind-hearted soul who had shaped her into the person that she had become. As she cared for him with unconditional love and devotion, she discovered a newfound strength within herself, forged in the fires of adversity and fueled by the enduring bond between a granddaughter and her beloved grandpa.

In the end, Lewis might have lost his battle with Alzheimer's, but his legacy lived in the hearts of those who loved him. Belle, Adam, and Kathy were forever changed by the experience of caring for him, their lives enriched immeasurably by the lessons of love, resilience, and compassion that he had taught them.

Then, he left. He was gone. Her world was turned upside down again. He left, just like her biological father at six weeks old; he left just like her childhood best friend at eight. He left just like her grandmother did in 2006. He left just like everyone always does. This made her feel guilty for months.

This was the worst day of her life. Or so she thought.

❖

In October of 2021, Adam reached out for help in his recovery. Belle's heart sank as she watched Adam drive away, leaving behind their home and their family to seek help at a detox facility. She knew it was the right decision for him, but the weight of suddenly being responsible for raising their two young boys alone felt overwhelming. As days turned into weeks, Belle found herself grappling with a whirlwind of emotions. She felt a deep sense of loneliness without Adam by her side, coupled with fear and uncertainty about the future. The mental struggles she faced seemed too great to overcome at times, threatening to consume her in a tide of despair.

But Belle refused to let herself drown. She knew that she had to be strong for her boys, to provide them with the love, stability, and support they needed during this challenging time. And so, she summoned every ounce of strength within her and set about comforting her boys in the best way that she knew how. She held them close, soothing their fears and wiping away their tears with gentle words and tender embraces. She read them bedtime stories, sang them songs, and tucked them in at night with assurances that everything would be okay. Belle also needed to maintain a sense of normalcy for her boys, sticking to their routines as much as possible and keeping them busy with activities they enjoyed. She took them to the park, baked cookies with them in the kitchen, and helped with homework. But even as she focused on comforting her boys, Belle couldn't shake the nagging doubt and worry that gnawed at her from within. She wondered if she was strong enough to handle the challenges of single parenthood, if she could provide for her boys emotionally and financially on her own. Yet, through it all, Belle drew strength from the love she had for her boys and the unwavering support of her family and friends. She leaned on them for guidance and encouragement.

And slowly but surely, Belle began to find her footing. She discovered reserves of resilience and courage within herself that she never knew she possessed, learning to navigate the ups and downs of parenthood with grace and determination.

Though the road ahead would be challenging, Belle knew that as long as she had her boys by her side, she could face whatever the future held with strength and resilience. As she looked into their bright, hopeful eyes, she felt a renewed sense of purpose and determination to create a bright and happy future for them, no matter what obstacles lay in her path.

This was the worst day of her life. Or so she thought.

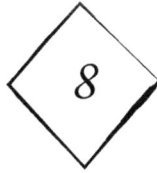

8

2022

March 26, 2022.

"What's your emergency?" asked the 911 operator.

"He's blue," said Belle. "He's not breathing. I can't find a pulse."

"Ma'am what's your address? Who's not breathing?"

"123 Willow Tree. My husband."

In the tense moment, Belle, desperate and determined, begins administering CPR to her husband, Adam. The room echoed with urgency as she recalled every step of her training. The rhythmic compressions were accompanied by a backdrop of fear and adrenaline. Time seemed to stretch.

"How close are they?? Are they almost here?" she asks though tears and labored breath.

"I will let you know when you need to stop and open the door."

Belle continued. Each compression an echo of hope. Belle's love propelled her though the harrowing experience, as she fought against the silence that threatened to engulf the room.

"Ma'am, they should be there any moment; they are on your street. You can stop and let them in."

"I can't stop. He's not back. He's still not breathing."

"Ma'am, it's okay; you have to let them in."

Belle continued to push deeply into her husband's chest. She looked down and realized that she was unclothed. Just a few short hours ago, she and Adam had been reminiscing about life. About how great things had been. She stopped and grabbed a long t-shirt and ran to the door, where police and paramedics were standing on the porch.

Belle pointed to the bedroom as they ran and continued where Belle had left off.

'Ma'am tell us about his history," said the EMT.

"He's healthy. No issues. I don't understand." As she fell to the floor, what felt like a ton of bricks fell into the pit of her stomach.

"He's in recovery for pills!" she yelled.

The first responders administered one dose of Narcan. Nothing. This was it. This was the worst day of her life. She was losing her king, the only man that had never left her. He was slowly leaving her. They administered another dose of Narcan. Adam took a deep breath, so deep she could hear him in the kitchen the next room over. She sighed the biggest sigh of relief followed by embarrassment, pain, and anger.

First responders got Adam up on the stretcher and wheeled him out of their bedroom, through the heart of their home, to the ambulance. They asked Belle if she could follow them to the hospital; she agreed.

Belle took a moment, walked back into the bedroom, looking at the bed, thinking to herself, What the fuck just happened? She started to look for clothes, as she needed to get to the hospital. She sat on the bathroom floor and called Linda.

Anxiety grips, lying face-down on the cold bathroom floor intensified the overwhelming experience of a panic attack. The cold tiles offered a sharp contrast to the heightened internal turmoil, creating a sensory clash. Each breath felt elusive, the surroundings blurry as distress amplified . The cold surface served as a grounding point, a tangible connection to relativity amid the emotional storm, yet the struggle persisted in the silence of the tiled space.

"Hello," said Linda.

"Linda, It's Adam; they took him. He's alive; they are on the way to the hospital. He overdosed."

"Where are you?" said Linda. "Breathe, honey; please breathe."

"I'm at home. On the bathroom floor."

"I'm on the way."

This was the worst day of her life. Or so she thought.

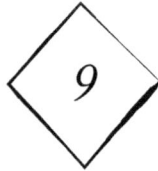

9

July 27, 2023

Today was the day that her youngest, Jackson, graduated preschool. It was a beautiful summer day. Belle dressed herself in her favorite navy dress with her new wedge shoes. She went to work like any other day. She drove to the hospital in Nashville. She pulled into the employee parking garage. She badged in. She drove from the first floor to the fourth floor, where she had to badge in again. She pushed her employee badge against the badge reader on the fourth floor and proceeded onto the seventh floor.

She texted Adam to let him know she had made it and grabbed her bags. It was just like any other day. The summer sun was shining in Nashville. Today was different. Her baby boy was graduating preschool.

Lunch time arrived. Belle messaged other members of her team to see if they were ready for lunch. She got a message from Jon, a tech that worked on the fifth floor. He was asking for assistance with the electronic medical record that Belle supported. She said she would be up shortly. Belle took the elevator to the fifth floor, which would be the last time, ever.

She got off the elevator and proceeded down the hallway. The tech and one of Belle's co-workers were behind a door that requireed a number to unlock. She entered the number to allow her entrance. Belle walked down a hallway, then turned to the left. She walked down another hallway into an office located to the right, where Jon and Allison were sitting. She said "hey" to both of them to not be rude.

Belle had told multiple members of leadership in the past that Jon showed narcissistic behaviors and she didn't feel comfortable working with him alone. They had brushed this off, saying, "Just don't go up there."

Jon needed assistance with installing the program that she supported. She provided this assistance. Once she finished, she let Allison know that it was time for lunch. They proceeded down the hallway and turned right to the next hallway. Jon called back to Belle, stating that he needed her admin login to complete the task.

Belle answered, "You don't need my log in."

"Yes, I do."

"Then it will have to wait until after lunch. Allison and I are headed down to the second floor for lunch."

They walked out into the hallway and proceeded to the elevator to take them to the hospital cafeteria. Belle received a call from her mother, Kathy, regarding the graduation tonight. Belle talked to her mother, making her way with Allison to the elevator.

Once in the elevator lobby, she saw Jon out of the corner of her eye, standing there waiting for her to get off the phone. She told her mother, " Hey, Mom, I have to go; I'll call you back." Belle hung up with her mother.

"What do you want??" she asked Jon.

"I really need your log-in credentials to get this application installed."

"No, you don't. We have the same access."

"Belle, yes, I do."

The elevator dinged letting them know that was there to take them down. Allison stepped into the elevator. Belle said to her, "I'll be right down; let me help him with this crap."

"Are you sure?"

"Yes; I will meet you in a few."

Belle followed Jon through the locked door, down the hallway. He turned left, heading to what she thought was the office. He stopped once he got to a supply room and pulled Belle in.

Belle was confused. "What are you doing?"

Jon tried to kiss her.

"Stop!" she said. "What are you doing?? You are being weird."

"Shut up. You know you like it."

"No! Stop! Please, what are you doing?!"

She grabbed her phone. She texted her best friend, Stephanie. Belle felt a mix of fear, panic, and desperation while her attacker was kissing her, especially since she was simultaneously texting her friend for help. She felt trapped, overwhelmed, and in desperate need of assistance to escape this. She could not do this alone.

Belle texted "HELP"

Steph: "Are you okay?"

Belle: "No. Fifth floor. Help me."

Belle clicked the side button on her phone, to turn the screen off. He stopped.

"What are you doing? I know you want this."

Jon proceeded to try and kiss her again. Belle put her hands on his chest and pushed him away. She was obviously terrified. "NO! STOP!" She thought she was yelling at him, but it was more of a whisper.

Jon turned Belle around and slammed her body against the wall. She says please no, stop. Jon continued to kiss her neck. He reached underneath her perfect navy dress. The one that she had picked to wear to Jackson's graduation. He moved her underwear to the side where she could feel that he was aroused by her. She was not feeling the same toward him.

Everyone says that in that moment they would fight. They would scream. They would demand that person to stop their unwarranted actions against them. Until it happens to you. You are screaming in your head, This is not happening. This does not happen to me. I told this man to stop. Why is he not listening to me? I am married. I am happy. Oh, God. Please. Please hear me. God, do you hear me? Please stop.

He didn't stop. He tried to place his penis into Belle. She stopped breathing. At that moment, that one split second, a man, a coworker, a friend, was taking everything she had worked for. He was taking away her peace. Her voice. He was taking her life.

She heard a door open. So did he. He stopped. She ran. She ran into someone. She said "sorry" and kept on running.

She ran into Stephanie in the hall. She knew. She could tell. She walked Belle back down to the first floor. Belle and she sat in the office while tears fell. "I said NO. I told him to stop."

Steph called one of their mutual friends. He immediately came down. He knew. He knew this man had hurt her. He had hurt her in ways that he could not explain. He told her, "Belle, we have to report it. You have to go now and report this." Belle was hesitant. She needed to call Adam. She knew that he would kill him. She said, "No. I can't report it."

He said "Let's go together; you don't have to do this alone. I will walk you. You will not be alone."

Belle and her friend Jacob walked across the campus to the director's office. Belle was not able to talk. She was in shock. The director heard her story. He immediately called the police. The metro police arrived, and Belle had to give her statement. She asked them if she could call Adam. It had been over an hour since the assault. In her head, she wanted movement before she called Adam.

It is hard to put into words just how overwhelming and frightening it is to report a sexual assault, especially considering it happened in her workplace. The thought of speaking up to someone who held power in the organization made her feel incredibly vulnerable and afraid of potential repercussions. Then the idea of involving the police added another layer of anxiety. Belle was terrified of not being believed or facing judgment during the investigation process. The thought of recalling the details of the assault that just took place, reliving that trauma, and navigating the legal system felt like an insurmountable challenge. The stigma and misconceptions surrounding sexual assault only intensified her fears. She worried about being blamed or dismissed, which made it harder to come forward. In those moments she felt isolated and alone. Unsure where to turn for support. It's crucial for workplaces and law enforcement agencies to create safe places for survivors like Belle to speak out without fear of retaliation or judgment. Having access to confidential support services and legal advocacy made a world of difference in her journey to seeking justice. But above all, what she needed most was to be heard, believed, and supported though every step of the process. Belle decided not to pursue charges against her attacker that day; the officers educated her that she could file them when she was ready.

Adam answered. "Hey"

"Babe, I'm okay," she said, starting to cry.

"Babe, what is it?"

"He assaulted me. The police are here. Please come now."

"WHO? Who did this? Where are you? I am on the way."

"I will explain everything when you get here. Please hurry."

This. This was the worst day in her life. This was the day that changed it all. The day that Belle immediately wanted to die. She was completely numb. She was ready to end it all. He took everything from her. He took her word. He took her soul. He took her will to live.

❖

Belle had always been a strong, independent woman. She had faced her fair share of challenges in life, but nothing could have prepared her for the horror she experienced that fateful day.

She wanted to scream, to run away and never look back, but she felt paralyzed by the trauma of what had just happened. In the days that followed, Belle's husband, Adam, was her rock. He held her close, comforting her with his presence and reassuring her that she was not alone.

Her life was shattered by this traumatic event. Sleep became a distant memory for her, elusive, as she lay awake, haunted by nightmares that seemed all too real. The comforting embrace of summer eluded her grasp, leaving her exhausted and weary.

Eating became a chore, each bite feeling like a burden too heavy to bear. Food lost its taste, its nourishment unable to penetrate the walls she had built around her wounded heart. The simple act of nursing herself became a battle against the memories that threatened to consume her.

Trust became a luxury she could no longer afford. Every person, every touch, felt like a potential threat, triggering a primal instinct to flee. The warmth of human connection was replaced by a cold, suffocating fear that left her isolated and alone. She tried to reassure herself, "I am safe." Like a desperate plea to a universe that had turned its back on her. But her body betrayed her, reacting with a visceral panic that left her trembling.

Together Adam and Belle sought help from a therapist, recognizing the importance of addressing the trauma head on and seeking professional support. Therapy became a lifeline for Belle, a safe space where she could unpack the trauma of her assault and begin the long and difficult journey of healing. With Adam by her side, she dove deep into her emotions, confronting the pain and fear that had been buried deep within her. It wasn't easy. There were days when Belle felt like giving up, when the weight of her trauma threatened to overwhelm her. But with Adam's unwavering support and the guidance of her therapist, she found the strength to keep going, to take one small step forward at a time. As Belle progressed in therapy, she began to realize that speaking up about her experience was not only important for her own healing but also for breaking the silence surrounding sexual assault.

10

Waking Up, But Wishing That You Don't

Belle found herself in a place of profound darkness, where the weight of despair seemed to crush her spirit. Each morning brought with it the struggles to even lift herself out of bed, let alone face the world outside. The temptation to succumb to the allure of self-harm whispered seductively in her mind, offering a twisted solace in the midst of her pain. This is what Adam feels. Finally, after all these years, she felt somewhat of an understanding. An understanding that the pills brought silence. Silence in the mind. Something she needed. Her body ached. Ached in a way that cannot be described. She was ready. Ready to end it all. Or so she thought.

In the depths of her despair, Belle discovered a flicker of resilience, a glimmer of hope that refused to be extinguished. Despite the overwhelming urge to give in to the darkness, she found the strength to resist. She knew, deep down, that she was worthy of love and happiness, even when it seemed so far out of reach. Belle always described it as a tunnel of darkness. That day she could see a glimpse of light at the end of that tunnel. She knew that light was warm, like summer. She could not give in.

Adam, her steadfast companion, stood by her side though it all.

Adam told her, "Babe, I not only have your six; I have your twelve, your three, and your nine. I will not only be ahead of you pulling you to me, behind you pushing you to succeed, but always beside you, with you through it all."

Despite their own struggles and the rocky terrain of their marriage, his love for Belle remained unwavering. He understood the depths of her pain, because he, too, had once been lost in the darkness. But together they found solace in each other's arms, a sanctuary from the storms raging within.

Their love, though tested by trials and tribulations, proved to be unbreakable. It was a beacon of light cutting through the shadows, guiding them through the darkest of nights. Through their shared journey of healing, they discovered that true love knows no bounds; it is a force powerful enough to conquer even the deepest of sorrows.

As Belle emerged from the darkness, she realized that her journey was far from over. But with Adam by her side, she knew that she could face whatever challenges lay ahead. Their love had weathered the storm, emerging stronger and more resilient than ever before. And in each other's embrace, they found the strength to conquer the darkness and embrace the light of a new day.

11

Her Inner Child

As Belle strolled through the Nashville suburb on a balmy spring day, the gentle breeze carried on the scent of blooming flowers. She noticed a mother and her daughter outside the daycare; as the little girl's laughter echoed in the air as she chased a butterfly. This place felt familiar to Belle. The sounds, the smells, even the view. The mother smiled warmly, her eyes reflecting the joy of watching her daughter explore the world around her. Belle couldn't help but feel a sense of warmth and contentment as she witnessed this simple yet beautiful moment of family bonding amidst the bustling suburban life.

Belle turned and walked to her car, turning her back to the family. She smiled reaching for the door handle, when she heard a scream. A scream described as a mother realizing that her child has disappeared. It is a sound of utter anguish and panic, a gut-wrenching cry filled with fear, desperation, and heartbreak. It's a sharp, piercing sound that cuts through the air, carrying with it the weight of a parent's worst nightmare come to life. In that moment, every fiber of her being is consumed by a primal instinct to find and protect her child, and her voice reflects the depth of her terror and agony.

"Where is she?!" screamed the mother.

Belle ran over to her. "What happened? She was right here?"

"I was grabbing her bag out of the car," said the mother, "and I dropped my phone! When I looked back, she was gone."

Belle's heart raced with urgency; she hurried across the street toward the pond, her footsteps quick and determined. With each step, the sound of gravel crunching beneath her feet echoed in the quiet suburban air. Reaching the pond's edge, she scanned its tranquil surface, her eyes darting back and forth in search of the missing child. With a gasp of horror, Belle's heart clenched as she noticed the child's motionless form floating facedown in the pond. Adrenaline surged through her veins as she sprinted toward the water's edge, her mind racing with fear and determination.

Without hesitation, Belle plunged into the pond, the cold water enveloping her as she swam toward the child. With each stroke, her arms strained against the resistance of the water, driven by an overwhelming sense of urgency and desperation.

Reaching the child, Belle gently lifted her limp body from the water, cradling her in her arms, With trembling hands she checked for signs of life, her heart pounding in her chest as she prayed for a response.

Through sheer determination and quick thinking, Belle administered CPR, her hands moving with practiced precision as she fought to revive the child. Moments later, as the child coughed and sputtered gasping for air, Belle's heart soaked with relief and gratitude.

Carrying the child to safety, Belle's eyes brimmed with tears of overwhelming emotion. In that moment, she knew that she had been given a second chance to ensure the safety and well-being of the precious life she now held in her arms.

As Belle rode in the ambulance with the frantic mother to the hospital, a heavy silence hung in the air, broken only by the sound of the siren wailing in the distance. The mother clutched Belle's hand tightly, her eyes filled with a mix of fear and hope as they sped through the streets.

Belle offered words of reassurance, her voice calm and steady, trying to provide whatever comfort she could in the midst of the chaos. She remained by the mother's side, offering support and solidarity, knowing that they were in this together.

Inside the ambulance, the sense of urgency was palpable, each passing moment feeling like an eternity as they raced against time to reach the hospital. Belle remained resolute, determined to do everything in her power to ensure the child's safety and well-being.

Together, Belle and the mother clung to hope, their shared determination forging a bond that would endure the most trying of circumstances. Belle didn't even know this mother, but there was something so familiar. As they finally arrived at the hospital, Belle stood ready to support the mother every step of the way, knowing that they would face whatever lay ahead together.

As Belle stepped out of the hospital, her heart still heavy with the weight of the day's events, she was met with a sight that took her breath away. The entire town had gathered outside. Their faces alight with relief and gratitude, the applause ringing out like a chorus of gratitude.

Tears welled up in Belle's eyes as she was enveloped by the warmth of their support, their cheers washing over her like a wave of reassurance and affection. She felt a sense of overwhelming gratitude for the community that had rallied around her in her time of need, their presence a reminder that strength could be found.

Amid the crowd, Belle spotted Adam. He stood waiting, his eyes shining with pride and admiration as he reached out to hold her in his arms. In that moment, as they held each other close, words seemed unnecessary, their love and gratitude communicated through the simple act of being together.

With Adam by her side, Belle felt a renewed sense of hope and purpose, knowing that no matter what challenges lay ahead, they would face them together. Belle took a deep breath, ready to embrace whatever the future held with courage and resilience.

As Belle awoke from her sleep, the remnants of the dream still lingered in her mind like wisps of fog slowly dissipating in the morning light. She took a deep breath, the sensation of peace and contentment from the dream still lingering within her. Reflecting on the dream, Belle felt a sense of clarity wash over her. It was a dream where she had confronted the wounds of her past, where she had found the courage to heal her inner child and embrace the fullness of her being.

Though it had only been a dream, Belle knew that its message was clear; she had the power within herself to overcome the pain of the past and embrace a future filled with hope and possibility. With a renewed sense of purpose, Belle rose from her bed, ready to face the day with a heart filled with gratitude and a spirit buoyed by the knowledge that she was on the path to healing and wholeness.

12

The Aftermath

In the months following the assault, Belle found herself navigating through a maze of emotions and challenges, trying to piece together her shattered sense of self. The support she expected from her workplace was disappointingly absent. Colleagues checked in briefly, offering superficial condolences before retreating back to their own lives, leaving Belle to grapple with her trauma. As she returned to work, Belle encountered a hostile environment that only exacerbated her pain. Forced meetings became a regular occurrence, where she felt scrutinized and accused, as if her assault tainted her credibility. The insidious whispers of jealousy and resentment from her coworkers poisoned the once-friendly atmosphere she had known. Her boss, Nathan, once a father figure who had guided and supported her, now turned a blind eye to her suffering, favoring another coworker without a second thought. The betrayal cut deep, leaving Belle feeling abandoned and betrayed once again.

Before the traumatic incident that had shaken Belle's world, the office dynamics had already been rife with tension. At one point, Belle and a coworker, Veronica, had been more than just colleagues; they had been friends. But something shifted; something sinister began to brew beneath the surface, poisoning their once-amicable relationship.

It all started when their boss, Nathan, began to show blatant favoritism toward Veronica. Belle couldn't ignore the subtle cues; the extra leniency about her not attending mandatory meetings, the coveted assignments handed to Veronica on a silver platter, while others, including Belle herself, were left to fend for scraps.

As the days turned into weeks and then months, Belle noticed the gradual transformation of her workplace into a battleground of egos and ambitions. Veronica's once-friendly demeanor morphed into a mask of superiority, her every interaction laced with condescension and thinly veiled hostility toward Belle. Despite her best efforts to maintain professionalism, Belle found herself on the receiving end of Veronica's venomous remarks and passive-aggressive behavior. Each encounter felt like a dagger aimed at her confidence and sense of belonging in the workplace.

Feeling isolated and betrayed, Belle made a crucial decision in April of 2023: to document every instance of mistreatment, every whispered insult, every slight, no matter how insignificant it seemed at the time. It was her way of reclaiming control in a situation where she felt powerless, a lifeline amidst the storm of uncertainty and fear. Little did Belle know that her documentation would become her strongest weapon in the battle for justice and redemption. But for now, as the tensions continued to simmer beneath the surface, she braced herself for whatever storm lay ahead.

But the ultimate betrayal came on her birthday, of all days, when her director met with her under the guise of celebration, only to accuse her of speaking out of line to the hospital staff, regarding the assault. The threat was clear: keep silent or face the consequences. It was a chilling reminder of the power dynamics at play and the lengths to which those in authority would go to protect their own interests.

The timing of the raise, coinciding with the director's demand for Belle's silence, raised significant suspicion. While the company might frame it as a gesture of appreciation or acknowledgement of her work, the context suggested otherwise. It is reasonable to interpret the raise as an attempt to buy Belle's compliance, essentially hush money disguised as an award. By offering financial incentive, the company might hope to dissuade Belle from speaking out and avoid further scrutiny or legal repercussions. Belle refused to be silenced or bought off, asserting her integrity and unwillingness to compromise her principles for the sake of appeasing those who had failed to support her in her time of need.

This was one of the worst days. Or so she thought.

Fury boiled within Belle as she navigated the treacherous waters for her workplace, feeling isolated and betrayed at every turn. The hollow condolences and fleeting check-ins from colleagues only served to deepen her sense of loneliness, leaving her to wrestle with her demons in the shadows of her own despair. In a place where healing should have been paramount, Belle found herself suffocating under the weight of distrust and suspicion. The very institution where she had sought solace and care had become a haunting reminder of her trauma, a betrayal of the sacred trust she had placed in its hands. Assaults were not supposed to happen in the sterile halls of a hospital; they were supposed to be confined to dark alleys or hidden corners, not lurking within plain sight in the walls of healing.

Yet there she was, forced to confront her pain in the very place it had been inflicted, surrounded by colleagues she could no longer trust. The realization cut deep, igniting a fiery rage within her as she grappled with the injustice of it all. How could they expect her to keep silent, to play along with their charade, when they had failed to protect her in the first place?

The anger burned bright within her, fueling her determination to break free from the suffocating silence that threatened to consume her. She refused to be silenced, refused to be complicit in their deceit. For Belle, the time for playing nice had long passed. It was time to reclaim her voice, to demand accountability, and to shatter the facade of indifference that had shielded her assailant from justice for far too long.

Belle's experience laid bare the harsh reality that many women face when confronting sexual assault; the pervasive culture of silence and disbelief that often leaves victims feeling isolated and powerless. It is a culture that prioritizes protecting institutions and perpetrators over supporting and believing survivors, perpetuating a cycle of pain and suffering. The fear of not being believed, or facing judgment and blame, of being retraumatized by the very systems meant to provide support, all contributes to the staggering number of sexual assault survivors who suffer in silence. It's a toxic cocktail of shame, stigma, and systemic failure that forces women into the shadows, where their pain festers and their voices are silenced. But Belle's story is also a testament to resilience and courage. Despite the overwhelming odds stacked against her, she refused to succumb to the silence. This went on for six long months. She demanded accountability. Her journey is a stark reminder that the path to healing begins with breaking the silence, with shining a light on the darkness that thrives in the shadows of indifference and complicity.

❖

As Belle sat in the sterile conference room, her heart sank with each word that Nathan and her director uttered. Their accusations felt like a betrayal, a twist of the knife in her already wounded spirit. They spoke of jealousy toward Veronica as if it were a crime, as Belle's perfectly valid concern about mistreatment and favoritism were nothing more than petty envy. Nathan's decision to halt the monthly newsletters, the daily inspirational messages, and the cherished team lunches felt like a punishment tailored specifically for Belle, a reminder of her perceived inadequacy in the eyes of her superiors.

And then there were allegations of her relationships being too casual, reported to HR by providers. Belle felt her cheeks flush with indignation. How dare they twist her professional interactions into something sordid and inappropriate? She had always conducted herself with integrity and respect, despite the toxic atmosphere that suffocated her in the workplace.

But what cut the deepest was their dismissal of her leadership abilities. They painted her as a follower, a subordinate incapable of leading her team to success. It was a slap to everything Belle had worked so hard to achieve, a denial of her potential and worth. What stung the most was their glaring omission; not once did they acknowledge the trauma that Belle had endured, the trauma that had haunted her every waking moment since that fateful day. They failed to recognize the signs of distress, the cry for help masked behind a facade of professionalism. If only they had listened to her months ago; if only they had taken her concerns about Jon seriously instead of brushing them aside. Maybe then, just maybe, Belle wouldn't be sitting here, branded as an underperforming, jealous female in need of etiquette classes.

As she left the conference room, the weight of their words heavy on her shoulders, Belle vowed to fight back, to reclaim her dignity and her voice in a world determined to shut her up. And though the road ahead seemed daunting, she refused once again to let it break her spirit. She was stronger than they ever could imagine.

13

Trials of Wyatt

Belle sat on her bed, the dim light casting shadows across her face as she flipped through a stack of papers—court documents, incident reports, and school disciplinary notices. Each one told a story of her son's descant into trouble, a journey she had feared but felt powerless to stop.

Wyatt, her beloved son, had always been a challenge. Spirited and headstrong, he had a knack for finding trouble where others saw only innocence. But three separate encounters with the law had shattered any illusion of innocence left in Belle's mind.

The first time was a blur of flashing police lights and tearful apologies. A petty theft, they said. A moment of foolishness that landed Wyatt in juvenile detention for a night. Belle had pleaded with the authorities to set her son straight, but deep down she knew it was only the beginning.

As Belle received the call from the principal's office, her heart sank. Another incident involving Wyatt, this time with drugs. It was a scene she had witnessed before, a painful echo of his father's past mistakes that haunted her every step.

Rushing to the school, Belle's mind raced with a whirlwind of emotions—anger, fear, disappointment. How did it come to this?

She had tried hard to steer Wyatt away from the dangers that lurked in the shadows, but it seemed her pleas had fallen on deaf ears.

As Belle and Adam sat across from the principal, his words hung heavy in the air. Wyatt had been caught with drugs on school property, a serious offense that left no room for negotiation. With a heavy heart, they listened as he outlined the consequences—expulsion, mandatory counseling, and a transfer to an alternative school for troubled teens.

Tears welled in Belle's eyes as she struggled to comprehend the gravity of the situation. Wyatt, her bright and promising son, now labeled as a delinquent, a statistic in a system that seemed determined to swallow him whole.

Again, Belle vowed to stand by her son, to fight for his redemption with every fiber of her being. She enrolled him in alternative school, determined to provide him with the support and guidance he so desperately needed. It wouldn't be easy. The road ahead would be paved with challenges and obstacles, but Belle refused to give in.

As Belle received the dreaded phone call yet again, her heart sank like an anchor into the depths of despair. Wyatt, her son, was in trouble with the law once more, this time involved in an altercation in the neighborhood. The news hit her with a force she had grown all too familiar with, a relentless barrage of pain and disappointment that threatened to engulf her.

The details of the altercation were murky, obscured by a haze of conflicting accounts and raw emotions. But one thing was clear: Wyatt was once again on the wrong side of the law, his future hanging in the balance like a delicate thread.

But even in the midst of her own turmoil, Belle refused to abandon Wyatt. Her family urged her to pay more attention to him. She had been. She was not going to abandon him, a lesson she had learned long ago, a lesson reinforced by every turbulent moment in her own life.

"You can't help them if you're not here." That's what a flight attendant would say if a plane was going down. You have to fit the oxygen mask over your own face. It was a simple truth, one she clung to as she navigated the turbulent air with Wyatt.

So she fought. She fought for Wyatt, for herself, for the promise of a better tomorrow. And though the road ahead was uncertain, she refused to give up hope. For in the depths of her despair, Belle once again found the strength to keep going, to keep fighting, to see loving her son through it all.

14

Charges Are Filed

With a steady resolve born from the months of suffering, Belle made the courageous decision to take matters into her own hands. No longer willing to be a passive victim of injustice, she picked up the phone and dialed the police department, her heart pounding with a mixture of fear and determination. As she spoke to the officer on the other end of the line, she felt a sense of empowerment swell within her. This was her moment to reclaim control, to demand accountability for the violation she had endured. Despite the gnawing ache for approval and validation, Belle knew that deep down remaining silent was no longer an option. The discomfort of speaking out paled in comparison to the suffocating silence she had endured for far too long.

A date was set for Belle to give her official statement, and though nerves threatened to betray her, she stood firm in her resolve. With each step she took toward the police station, she felt a weight lifting from her shoulders, replaced by a newfound sense of purpose and hope. In that moment Belle realized that she was no longer alone in her struggle. Yes, Adam has been here through it all. He never forced Belle to make this decision. He loved her. But she needed to tell her story to someone who could serve justice. Though the road ahead would undoubtedly be fraught with challenges and obstacles, she knew that she was no longer content to suffer in silence. She was ready to confront her attacker head on, to demand the justice she so rightfully deserved. And with that realization, Belle stepped into the police station, ready to speak her truth, ready to reclaim her power.

As Belle found herself thrust into the daunting world of the Special Victims Unit, she braced herself for the inevitable barrage of questions, judgments, and scrutiny that often accompanied such investigations. But to her surprise, what she encountered was not a cold, indifferent bureaucracy, but rather a team of dedicated professionals who treated her with the utmost respect and compassion. From the moment she walked through the doors of the office, Belle was greeted with kindness and empathy. The detectives listened attentively as she recounted the harrowing details of her attack, offering words of comfort and reassurance along the way. But it was their approach that truly set them apart. Instead of relegating Belle to the role of a passive observer, they empowered her to take control of the situation, to be the driving force behind redemption. They valued her unwavering determination to set things right.

With their guidance and support, along with Adam, Belle navigated the complexities of the legal system with confidence and grace. They kept her informed every step of the way, ensuring that she remained in the driver's seat. Again, the road ahead of her was fraught with challenges and uncertainties. Belle took solace in knowing that she had the SVU team by her side, steadfast allies in her quest for justice and redemption. For in a world filled with darkness and despair, there were always beacons of light, guiding her through another storm with unwavering compassion and respect.

Through it all, Belle learned that it was okay to speak up, to tell her story when she was ready, and to seek support from those who loved her. She discovered that healing was a journey, not a destination, and that with time and patience, she would find peace and healing. And though the scars of her assault would always be a part of her, Belle refused to let them define her. With Adam's love and support, she found the courage to reclaim her life, to stand tall in the face of adversity, and to emerge from the darkness stronger and more resilient than ever before.

If you or someone you know needs to speak with someone, there are people available 24/7.

National Sexual Assault Hotline: 1-800-656-4673
Substance Abuse and Mental Health Hotline: 1-800-662-4357
988 Suicide and Crisis Lifeline: SMS 988

Additionally, I am available for inquiries via email at sophiawells.author@gmail.com

Epilogue

As I reach the final pages of my journey, I pause and reflect on the journey that I have shared with you. It has been a tumultuous ride, filled with highs and lows, triumphs and setbacks. But through it all I find solace that I am not alone. I hope my words resonate with you, offering comfort, guidance, and hope in your time of need.

To all who have followed me on this journey, I thank you from the bottom of my heart. Your support has meant more to me than you'll ever know. Don't suffer in silence. If no one else is listening, know that I am. Your voice matters, and I am here to listen.

I know far too well the power of a sympathetic ear and having someone on your side in this time of need. So I extend this offer to my readers, a beacon of light in a world too often shrouded in darkness.

It is a reminder that the burden of change should not rest solely on the shoulders of survivors. It is a call to action for society as a whole to dismantle the systems of oppression and injustice that enable sexual assault violence to flourish. Only then can we hope to create a world where women no longer suffer alone in silence.